# Hearts & Soul

# Faith and Finance

Jane L. Fryar

Jennifer Henry

Patricia R. Mitchell

Kimberly Ingalls Reese

Linda Schulenburg

Cynda Strong

CPH®

Concordia Publishing House

Edited by Jane L. Fryar

This publication is available in braille and in large print for the visually impaired. Write to Library for the Blind, 1333 S. Kirkwood Road, St. Louis, MO 63122-7295; or call 1-800-433-3954.

# Contents

## Leader Guide

# Money Matters

## Ice Breaker (10 minutes)

List five things you value most. Rank them in numerical order, with **number one** representing your most treasured possession. Then explain to your group why you listed the things you did.

## Money—Gift of God (20 minutes)

How freely do you discuss financial issues? For instance, does your best friend know what you earn? Do your co-workers know about your retirement savings plan or what you pay in rent?

Most people consider personal finances a private matter. Few of us broadcast information about our bank balances or credit card debt. In fact, many people discuss their use of Viagra or hormone replacement therapy more freely than they reveal information about their personal spending habits.

Then, too, many Christians consider financial planning and the use of money somehow unworthy of our calling as Christ's people. Hasn't God called the love of money "a root of all kinds of evil" (1 Timothy 6:10)? Even so, we find ourselves at times yearning for more money and for the things it can buy. We even fall for the temptation to believe that money can provide the security we crave. Still, we know that God's gift of salvation far exceeds in value any earthly treasure.

So what are we to make of all this? How do we deal with all these seeming contradictions and with our conflicting thoughts and feelings? More important, what has our Savior-God told us?

1. According to Genesis 1 and 2, God gave His human creations all that we need. Look at Genesis 2:8–14. Adam and Eve lived in a perfect state before sin. The Lord provided for all their needs.

a. How does the creation account confirm the goodness of God's physical creation?

b. God likes physical matter; He created it! When does appreciating created things become sin? In other words, when does appreciating material things become materialism? See Romans 1:25; Romans 7:7–8; Ephesians 5:5; and 1 Peter 5:6–7.

2. Most of us know all this, yet we nonetheless struggle with money issues. Read the descriptions below. Which of these women do you most closely identify with? Explain as much as you can comfortably share.

- Cara, with a new business degree, seems headed for a bright career. Still, she has accumulated student loans and credit-card debt buying necessities like books and clothing. Now she deals with stress as she attempts to organize her bills and begin her career.
- Sally, a single mom, struggles to make ends meet. She works to support her two small children but lives barely above a subsistence level. She wants her children to have what their friends have.
- Mary's marriage suffers because of credit-card debt and various loans. Constant stress and arguing over finances disrupt the peaceful, secure family life she craves.
- Wendy has a great career. Her recently deceased husband left a large estate. People wonder why she still works, and it seems nearly everyone wants a piece of her wealth.
- Single and independent, Irene faces some frightening prospects. According to her doctor, her recent bouts with forgetfulness and fatigue present cause for concern. He has recommended that she begin to look for an assisted-living facility. Her meager Social Security check and her small savings account will not buy the care she may soon need.

## Financial Pitfalls (20 minutes)

Many of us find it difficult to surrender our finances completely to our Lord. Often greed or worry controls us. We base our self-worth on buying things and owning stuff. We struggle with fears and insecurities as we think about the future.

1. When do you find it most difficult to surrender money issues to God?

2. In making, spending, saving, or giving money, God wants us to look to Him for wisdom and security. Yet all too often we convince ourselves we know more. We doubt God's care for us. The words of 1 Peter 1:18–21 present the Good News using a word picture drawn from economics.

a. Identify that word picture, then apply it to your sins of worry, greed, covetousness, and any other sin-debts you have identified as you've worked through this session.

b. Read Matthew 10:29–31. How do these words calm your worries and make it possible for you to trust God with your finances?

## Financial Planning (5 minutes)

God gives all good things—including our money and our possessions. He intends them for our good, for our enjoyment (1 Timothy 6:17). Free in Christ and His cross, we can use these blessings to honor Him.

In the week ahead, gather your financial records and evaluate your position. Identify and quantify your debts. List predictable future needs. Consider any saving or investing strategies you've begun. Think about your giving habits. Do all this in the shadow of Christ's cross, as it were. Remember that your Savior sits beside you at your desk or kitchen table. Prayerfully consider any changes you might want to make—even if you have no idea right now how to make them. We will return to these challenges in the weeks ahead.

## Conclusion

Sing or say together stanza 4 of Martin Luther's "A Mighty Fortress Is Our God" (*Lutheran Worship* 298) as you close.

*Dear Father, give us strength in all our dealings with money to see it as a gift from You to use to Your glory. May we earn it, spend it, save it, and give it away with zeal and cheerful hearts. May we always remember that our greatest gift, our salvation, came at great cost to You—the lifeblood of Your only Son. Still, You gave it freely. The comfort and security we long for are found only in this Treasure. Thank You, Father! In Jesus' name. Amen.*

# Making Money

## Ice Breaker (5 minutes)

Down through history, people have created ways to trade and barter for things they may need or want. Animal pelts, gold coins, and paper money have all served this purpose. Today all kinds of electronic transactions have replaced earlier methods of exchanging value. Regardless of the forms money takes, what kinds of challenges can making money present?

## Financial Lifestyle (15 minutes)

People deal with money in four basic ways.

• We make it.

• We spend it.

• We save it.

• We give it.

1. Consider the ladies from our previous session. Which of them would most likely focus on issues of making money? Explain.

• **Cara**—College grad, career-minded, credit-card poor

• **Sally**—Single, struggling mom

• **Mary**—Married, maxed-out credit

• **Wendy**—Widowed, wealthy

• **Irene**—Ill, ill-at-ease

2. What issues of *making* money challenge you?

## *Money-Making and Its Meaning (15 minutes)*

Most people work to earn money or some sort of compensation. Compensation varies from job to job and place to place, but Scripture applies general guidelines to all kinds of work.

1. Summarize 2 Thessalonians 3:6–15 and Colossians 3:23–24.

a. How do Paul's words dignify all work, no matter what the monetary compensations?

b. Given this dignity, how can you characterize the work you do as a "vocation"—your God-given "calling"? What encouragement does that provide?

2. Despite the dignity Scripture assigns to all honest labor, compensation issues can cause us to demean our work and our ways of making money. For instance, in our world, people often equate work and worth. A pro-basketball player makes enough money to pay cash for a 17,000-square-foot home. A grocery clerk earns minimum wage and rents a 700-square-foot home.

a. Which of these people is worth more?

b. When might you be tempted to measure your worth by your salary or the size of your stock portfolio?

3. What else does making money mean to you?

a. For instance, would you take a low-paying job if you saw it as a way to fulfill God's calling to serve others? Would you take a high-paying, high-pressure job if you saw it as your God-given vocation or calling? Explain.

b. Have you always given "a full-day's work" for "a full-day's pay"? Explain.

4. Think about the issue you just discussed. What less-than-God-pleasing attitudes or behaviors did you discover?

## My Savior, My Worth (15 minutes)

Regardless of what your employer, your bank, or your neighbors think of your worth, the sinless Son of God died for you. A rule of thumb in business dictates that "a thing is worth what someone will pay for it." By that standard, your worth is astronomical, even infinite!

1. Study Ephesians 1:1–14.

a. With what word pictures drawn from the realm of economics does this passage describe your worth?

b. Which words make it clear that you did not earn your salvation or make yourself worthy?

2. Reread the text.

a. In what ways do these truths challenge your ideas about the money you make or the work you do?

b. How can the truths here transform your worries about not making enough money?

## *Financial Planning (5 minutes)*

After today's class session ends, think through the personal financial details you have accumulated so far. If you need to save more, consider specific lifestyle changes that could make that possible. If your savings and investing strategies seem adequate already, prayerfully consider changes you might make to reflect better stewardship of the dollars the Lord has entrusted to your care.

## *Conclusion (5 minutes)*

Close your study by singing or reading the four stanzas of "Lord, to You Immortal Praise" (*LW* 496).

*Dear Father, thank You for all that I have and am through Christ. Help me to do the work You have given me to the best of my ability, knowing that I serve the Lord Christ. Also teach me to use my financial resources wisely. In Jesus' name I pray. Amen.*

# Spending Money

## Ice Breaker (5 minutes)

Last time we introduced the idea that we relate to money in four basic ways: we make it, spend it, save it, and give it. This session will focus on ways we spend what we make.

As you begin, use a chalkboard or a large piece of paper to list some of the ways money can be spent or misspent. Mention situations you have heard or read about, but avoid confessing others' sins! If you feel comfortable doing so, share a spending struggle you once faced or now face.

## Toys, Trust, and Trinkets (10 minutes)

Ads, billboards, television commercials, and pop-up windows on the Internet all urge us to buy, buy, buy. Advertisers, with glitz and regularity, push products on us we never knew we needed. Soon these things become must-haves in our household. And it's easy to buy—no money now! Low credit terms! Bad credit? No credit? No problem! Meanwhile, too many of us work longer and harder to pay for things we have little time to enjoy.

This session asks us to consider how we spend money. Where do we spend it? What do we spend it on? Why? Once we answer those questions, we'll look at them in the light of God's Word to us. Then we can better evaluate our spending decisions.

- "I make an okay salary," college-grad Cara says, "but my college loans take a colossal bite out of it. I have 10 years of payments ahead of me. I want to save for a down payment on a house, and I want to take a trip to Europe with my girlfriends this summer. I'm thinking of getting a second job in the evenings and on week-ends." On the basis of what she figures she'll earn working three evenings a week and all day Saturday at a clothing store near her apartment, Cara has begun planning in earnest for her trip, and tomorrow she will visit a real estate agent to talk about a condo.
- "There's More Month Than Paycheck" could be struggling-mom Sally's theme song. She finds herself torn between buying

household essentials and giving her kids the things they want. She pays the rent on time—most of the time—but her utility bills usually run a little late. She keeps on top of her credit cards by paying the minimum amount required each month. She reserves some cash from each paycheck so she and the kids can treat themselves to a meal out once a week—it's one of the very few luxuries she allows herself. "It's a juggling act," she says. "I know I should save something, and I should give something to church, but I just can't do it right now. Maybe next year."

• "We both earn good salaries, and besides, I like to shop," says maxed-out Mary of her spending habits. "A credit card balance is just a fact of life." Mary takes pride in her pricey home and trendy clothes—"When I see just the right thing for the house or for my wardrobe, I buy it." A couple she knows takes weekend getaways at a nearby resort. They have invited Mary and Phil to go with them next time, but Phil is adamant—"We just can't afford it!"

• Wealthy Wendy's comfortable circumstances have allowed her to cultivate what her friends call "exquisite taste." Her clothes are not flashy, but neither does she buy them at discount department stores. The waiters in at least one upscale restaurant know her by name. Wendy enjoys their approval when she chooses one of the best wines to complement her carefully selected appetizer and entrée. "I like being a snob," she laughs. Wendy spends generously on gifts for her friends and gives money to charity each Christmas. She describes her attitude toward money as "sophisticated."

• As she considers how to afford the help she needs with her illness, Irene insists on going it alone. She hasn't yet told her children about her doctor's diagnosis or advice. When she learned how much residential care would cost in a nearby home for the elderly, Irene panicked. She's crying herself to sleep at night, and she almost bought cans of cat food instead of tuna for herself when she got groceries this weekend.

*When you think about the ways you **spend** money, with which of these women do you most closely identify? Why?*

## *Money, Greed, Worry (15 minutes)*

1. Read 1 Kings 10:14–29, the account of Solomon's wealth. Oriental custom measured a king's power by the splendor of his palace and the opulence of his lifestyle.

a. In what ways did Solomon use his wealth to the glory of the God of Israel?

b. In what ways did King Solomon's spending dishonor the God of Israel? Compare Deuteronomy 17:14–20.

2. Shortly after Solomon's death, his kingdom split into two parts—north and south, Israel and Judah. The kings continued to live in luxury, benefiting from Solomon's many trade agreements with neighboring nations. Wealthy cities arose in both Judah and Israel, and the people prospered. That is to say, they prospered materially.

a. Read Amos 4:1–5, and describe what happened spiritually.

b. Why do you think the prophet singled out women in particular for the condemnation recorded here?

3. Someone has said, "God doesn't mind if we have things—He just doesn't want things to have us!" When do "things have us"? How can we diagnose this?

4. Go back over the list you made at the beginning of this session and identify the misspending you noted.

a. How many of these problems can you trace back to greed?

b. Where has greed shown up in your own life as you think about how you spend money?

5. Sally and Irene, especially, seem more prone to worry than to greed.

a. How does Jesus address this sin in Matthew 6:25–34?

b. When does worry about money issues plague you?

## *Return to the Lord Your God (20 minutes)*

Amos traveled throughout Israel warning the people of God's judgment. He begged them to return to the Lord their God in repentance. Along with the words of solemn warning we read earlier, the prophet offered words of hope.

1. Read Amos 9:11–15.

a. Here Amos uses picture language. What does he describe?

b. God's forgiveness in Christ's cross restores our "broken places"—including places broken by a false relationship with money. How does this comfort you and bring peace?

2. In Isaiah 33:6, the Lord promises His people "a treasure." How does it differ from the "treasures" we buy or want to buy? In what ways is it infinitely better?

## Financial Planning (5 minutes)

Look through your check stubs and the stack of financial documents you have been gathering. Identify specific issues that arise due to greed or worry. Confess these sins to your Lord. Then, confident in Christ's cross, ask the Holy Spirit to change your attitudes and habits. Be specific about the changes. Name them, then ask Him! See Matthew 7:7–8.

## Conclusion

Sing "Take My Life, O Lord, Renew" (*LW* 404) as a prayer of praise and petition to God, who has given us all things to use for His glory and for our own and our neighbor's good.

*Heavenly Father, Your Son died for my sin. He is my highest, greatest treasure. Forgive me for my sins of unbelief, greed, and worry. Forgive my skewed priorities and my reliance on money for security. Give me faith to trust in You for every good; Your steadfast love endures forever! Amen.*

# Saving Money

## Ice Breaker (10 minutes)

Think back a moment. Back to the days before you could use a credit card—maybe even all the way back to childhood. Think about a time you saved your money for something you really wanted. You earned it, you counted it, and you waited for weeks or even months until finally you had enough. Off to the store you went, coming home with your prize in hand.

Share that process and the sense of accomplishment you felt.

## Saving or Stockpiling (10 minutes)

When asked how much money is enough, John David Rockefeller is said to have replied, "Just a little more." Doesn't that ring true? How often do we think, "If only I had a little more, then I could save. I could get that new car. I could take that vacation"?

Rockefeller was not the first person to notice this tendency in sinful hearts. In fact it predates him by many years. King Solomon noted it in Ecclesiastes 5:10:

> *Whoever loves money never has money enough;*
> *whoever loves wealth is never satisfied with his income.*
> *This too is meaningless.*

The unquenchable thirst for just a little more has another name: hoarding. On the other hand, diligently saving for a rainy day, a special family vacation, or even for retirement can be very rewarding. It builds patience. It teaches self-control and puts the brakes on impulsive spending. It brings satisfaction when you at last reach your goal. So when does saving become hoarding?

Here are five Christian women who struggle with issues of saving and hoarding money:

- Still confident with the idea that she will have plenty of time later, Cara spends everything she earns. She used her sign-on bonus as a down payment on a car. Now, the cumulative effect of that loan, her student loans, and her credit-card debt have made her ineligible for a home loan, even though she wants very much to buy a house. Considering the 20 percent she would have to put down for a conventional loan, she's started to look at other options—an FHA loan or one of those special deals local builders of condos are offering.

• When asked about saving money, Sally just laughs. "How can you save anything when the kids need new shoes and the electric bill comes due? There just isn't anything left over." To cover necessities, Sally often uses her credit cards. Secretly she worries about getting sick and losing her job. The old adage "just one paycheck away from the poor house" fits Sally's situation uncom - fortably well.

• Mary and her husband, Phil, both have retirement accounts at work. They have also established a small slush fund to cover emergencies. If they paid off their credit cards and stopped impulse buying, they would have even more money to put away, but Mary resists Phil's pressure to do this. She accuses him of wanting to squirrel away every dime, while he resents her burning through most of what they both work so long and hard to earn.

• Wendy doesn't save, she invests. She manages her portfolio care fully. If an investment does not make money after a reasonable time period, she moves it. Once she has earmarked dollars for investing, Wendy almost never spends it. Very disciplined with her money, Wendy wants to be prepared for anything.

• Irene wishes she and her husband had saved more for retirement. She also regrets their divorce. Coming as it did in the heady days of the late 1960s, the divorce had seemed right at the time. How had those song lyrics gone? "I am woman; hear me roar!" Irene no longer feels much like roaring. Rather, she watches in silence, helpless to keep the ripples of past mistakes from washing over her life and eroding her security.

*When you think about your personal saving habits, which of these women do you more closely identify with? Explain your choice.*

## A Foolish Man, A Wise Woman (15 minutes)

1. Luke 12:13–21 and Proverbs 31:10–31 present an interesting study in contrasts. Both individuals had wealth and diligently oversaw

it. Both directly managed their financial issues day-to-day. Both looked ahead and had long-term goals. Yet the outcomes differed vastly. Read both texts, looking for these outcomes.

a. What differences do you see?

b. How do you account for them?

c. For what exactly does Jesus condemn the rich man?

d. The sins that overcame the rich man can tempt us as well. What temptations to hoard do you face?

2. Now turn back to the woman in Proverbs.

a. For what exactly did King Lemuel commend this woman?

b. The woman Lemuel describes has a heart of service. How does her reverence for the Lord, Israel's covenant God, shape who she is?

c. Suppose credit cards had been available. What would have been her attitude toward them? Under what circumstances might she have spent next week's money today? Explain.

3. Think about the wise woman of Proverbs 31 and the foolish man of Luke 12.

a. In what ways do you resemble each of these two money managers?

b. To what sins of omission and commission in your own lifestyle do these accounts point?

## Conceal or Confess (15 minutes)

Thankfully this study doesn't stop with the recognition of our shortcomings in regard to money management. Isn't it wonderful we don't have to rely on our wits and wiles to find our own way through the money maze?

1. What promises does our Lord make in Proverbs 28:13–14?

2. We do not face our selfishness or fears or frustrations alone. Jesus is our Savior and the Lord of our salvation. We can bring our dilemmas and fears to the cross. There we find forgiveness for our worrying, our selfishness, our hoarding, and our wastefulness. How does that forgiveness make it possible to start afresh each new day? See Psalm 51, especially verses 10–12.

3. We can trust our Lord to create pure hearts in His people and to grant us spirits willing to live in love and obedience to Him. What specific changes will you ask the Holy Spirit to work in you today?

## Financial Planning (5 minutes)

This week, consider the financial data you have already accumulated. What questions come to mind? List as many as you can. Then categorize them based on how you propose to find answers. Perhaps some questions call for further research on your part. Check your public library or explore Web sites on the Internet. Make sure the sources you consult have credibility. Don't act on any advice unless you verify it thoroughly—with someone you trust.

To tackle other questions, you may need professional advice. Many cities and towns have credit-counseling services available for free or at a minimal cost. Your pastor may know about reliable services in this regard. Many insurance companies and brokerage houses offer free financial assessments, but keep in mind that many times they are in business to sell products. Some financial planners work for a fee, often a percentage of their clients' assets. You need to weigh the advantage of their independent counsel against the cost of their service. Check with the Better Business Bureau before you settle on an advisor. Your tax professional may be able to refer you to a reputable advisor.

After you've formulated and categorized your questions, take out your calendar. Mark specific plans for finding answers. Schedule trips to the library and phone calls to your accountant. Do something every week to help yourself grow in the knowledge you need to steward the financial resources God has given you.

## Conclusion (5 minutes)

The woman described in Proverbs 31 exemplifies a servant's heart. She seeks first the Lord's kingdom and His righteousness (Matthew 6:33). He will also take care of tomorrow.

Sing stanzas 1 through 4 of "Oh, How Great Is Your Compassion" (*LW* 364) as you close.

*Dear Lord, thank You for Your love and concern about everything in our lives. We want to seek You and Your righteousness first in all we do. Teach us how to do that as we save and use the money You have given us. Do Your work in us today. In Jesus' name. Amen.*

# Giving Money

## Ice Breaker (10 minutes)

Think about the most generous person you've ever known. Tell why you chose that particular person. Was the person generous with assets other than money—time, for example? Did the person show wisdom in his/her generosity? Explain.

## Giving Money (10 minutes)

As you worked through previous sessions in this course, you probably noticed that, for most people, making, spending, and saving money mean more than simply the raw purchasing power money represents. For some, money reflects status and a sense of personal importance. Other people see money as a way to keep score in the great game of business. Some people look to their money for security. Still other folks save or invest in hopes of amassing enough dollars someday to free themselves from debt or from the need for a job.

Similarly, people assign various meanings to the act of giving money. Consider the five women we've discussed in previous sessions:

• Cara seldom thinks about giving. She does buy Girl Scout cookies each year, and she also stuffs several dollar bills into the Salvation Army kettle outside the mall at Christmastime. Then, too, when Cara sits down to pay bills, she usually remembers to write a check to her church—if she has enough left over. Cara sees herself as generous, or at least as generous as most people her age.

• Sally dedicates much of her money for giving—mostly giving to her children. Though not consciously aware of it, she expects their love and loyalty in exchange for her sacrifices on their behalf. Sally wishes she had more to give to church and to charity, but for now groceries come first. Somewhat like Cara in this regard, Sally waits to see what's left over at the end of the month and gives part of that.

• Mary cultivates an image of generosity with her friends. Her husband, Phil, and she often quarrel over the lavish gifts Mary insists on buying for weddings, birthdays, Christmas, and the like.

Futhermore, Mary would like to give 10 percent of the family income to their church, but Phil throws a fit. He sees it as wasteful, just another example of Mary's cavalier attitude toward money.

• Wendy's biggest money problems revolve around giving. To whom or what should she give? How generous should she be, can she be, without damaging initiative and wise stewardship in the planning processes of others—particularly her children and grandchildren? Wendy also worries about how much of her estate to give to her congregation. She's seen endowment money hurt other churches, and she doesn't want this to happen to hers.

• Irene gives generously—beyond what she is truly able to give—and has done so all her life. Her giving exemplifies the "widow's mite" extolled by Jesus in the Gospels. Lately, though, as Irene has faced her financial challenges, she has noticed a change in her attitude. She wonders if she is giving in an attempt to manipulate her Lord—to make Him somehow more responsive to her prayers for help.

*As you think about each person described above, with whom do you most closely identify? Explain as you feel comfortable sharing your thoughts.*

## Stingy, Foolish, Generous (15 minutes)

When Christians think about giving, they usually focus on giving as it relates to the work of the Lord, either through their local congregation or through some other Christian agency. Scripture has much to say about this.

1. Read one or more of the texts referenced below. How does each describe our heavenly Father's generosity?

a. Psalm 103

b. Matthew 5:44–45

c. 1 Timothy 6:17

2. Compare Proverbs 22:9 with 22:16. Summarize the limits to generosity Solomon suggests.

3. Read James 2:14–16 and 5:1–5. How does the apostle describe sins of selfishness in these verses?

4. Based on the texts you have read so far, discuss these questions:

a. What makes people stingy with their money? When does selfishness say no?

b. What leads people to give foolishly? When does foolishness say yes?

c. When do you struggle with sins of selfishness or foolishness in your own giving?

## *The Generous Grace of God (15 minutes)*

Despite our sins of selfishness and our foolish use of our Father's gifts to us, He continues to lavish His goodness on us. He forgives our sins in Christ and invites us to imitate Him in generosity and wisdom.

1. Read Titus 2:11–14 and 3:3–8.

a. How do these passages describe the generous grace of God toward you?

b. How does the new identity God gave you in your Baptism (Titus 3:5–6) produce a wise and generous lifestyle?

2. In 2 Corinthians 9, the apostle Paul presents a kind of case study in giving—giving motivated by God's lavish grace.

a. What verse(s) in particular highlight that grace?

b. What verse(s) hint at the need for wisdom in giving?

c. What promises does Paul attach to generosity?

## *Financial Planning (5 minutes)*

Prayerfully look once again at the financial records you've gathered in previous weeks.

- What information, advice, or help have you already gotten?


- What additional help do you need?


- This week think particularly about estate planning—whatever your age or financial resources. How can you show both wisdom and generosity as you think through issues of insurance, drawing up or amending your will, or setting up a trust?


## *Conclusion*

Together speak or sing the words of stanza 4 of the hymn "Take My Life, O Lord, Renew" (*LW* 404).

*Heavenly Father, You have, in love, generously given Your only Son into death for my sins. Transform my heart by Your grace so that I may learn to give more wisely and more generously. In Jesus' precious name. Amen.*

# Seeking First the Kingdom

## Ice Breaker (10 minutes)

Sometimes in a store or restaurant a friend will say to us, "Your money is no good here." What do they mean? Has anyone ever said this to you? Describe the experience.

## Cara, Sally, Mary, Wendy, Irene, and Me (10 minutes)

Choose one of the women we have met in this course. Or consider your own struggles with money management as you have analyzed them in the past several weeks and have discussed issues related to getting, spending, giving, and saving money. Jot a "talking points" memo you could use to guide a discussion with one of these women—or yourself—based on this course. For right now, use only Law. What attitudes and decisions need to be confronted? What sins need to be confessed? Summarize these in the space below. Base your summary on the descriptions given in sessions 1–5 in this course.

## Come to the Wedding! (15 minutes)

You have been invited to the wedding. Not the wedding of the decade. Not even the wedding of the century. Despite your sinful attitudes, your omissions, and your sinful actions in using money, you have been invited to the wedding of all weddings—the wedding banquet of Christ, the Bridegroom, and the Church, His bride. Like Cara, Sally, Mary, Wendy, and Irene, you need a new dress, as it were. Yet God has told you, "Your money is no good here."

1. Read the following passages, and explain what it means to know your money is no good to God.

a. Isaiah 52:3

b. Isaiah 55:1

2. Now describe the wedding, based on the passages below.

a. Revelation 19:7

b. Revelation 22:17

3. If your money is no good to God, how will you buy the clothes required for the wedding banquet? Read Matthew 22:1–14.

## The Lord, My Source (20 minutes)

The Law always accuses. When we face up to our own failures to obey our Lord and to honor Him in our financial decisions, we can easily despair. Or we can decide to exercise such personal discipline through sheer willpower that we do better—at least outwardly. Yet such efforts are doomed to produce even more despair or its evil twin—spiritual pride—in our hearts.

Still, in Christ and in the forgiveness of sins He obtained for us, we have hope. The Gospel is "the power of God for the salvation of everyone who believes" (Romans 1:16). Through that Gospel, God works in us all the attitudes, desires, and behaviors we cannot create by our own efforts.

1. Because this is true, savor the promises God makes in the verses referenced below. What comfort and hope do you find in each?

a. Colossians 3:12

b. Philippians 2:5–13

c. Philippians 4:4–7, 12–13

d. Ephesians 1:15–23; 3:14–21

2. In what ways is your life enriched by these promises?

3. Based on those promises and on all you've learned in other lessons of this course, what do you need God to do for you? Continue the "talking points" memo you began earlier, but this time add the transformational power Your Savior-God applies through the Gospel. Consider adding to that memo thoughts stimulated by the questions below:

a. For what sins do you need forgiveness? 1 John 1:8–9

b. With what fears do you need help? Matthew 10:29–31

c. For what worries do you need hope? Matthew 6:31–34

d. With what lifestyle changes do you need wisdom? James 1:5

e. To which people, agencies, or counselors could you turn for help with practical concerns? Proverbs 1:1–7

f. What prayer, encompassing these needs, can you offer in light of God's promise in Philippians 4:19?

## Financial Planning (5 minutes)

What further or ongoing plans can you make based on the beginning you have made during this course? How will you, by grace, move ahead with those plans?

## Conclusion

We earn, we save, we spend, and we give. We are hard working, diligent, cautious, and generous. How do we differ from non-Christians who do the same things? Many non-Christians handle their money very well, but in the end, they will learn that their money is no good to God. Only the robe of righteousness Christ Jesus earned for us on His cross will make us fit to attend the eternal marriage supper of the Lamb.

Nonetheless, in Christ—by faith in Him—our getting, saving, spending, and giving do honor our Lord. Christ Jesus sets us free from worry and greed, selfishness and the temptation to hoard, covetousness and idolatry. Furthermore, He wants to give us peace as we deal with every financial challenge and blessing in our lives. We can count on Him to do it because we know He has already given us the most beautiful gown imaginable, the robe of righteousness He won for us on His cross. See you at the wedding!

*Let us rejoice and be glad and give Him glory!*
*For the wedding of the Lamb has come,*
*And His bride has made herself ready.*
*Fine lines, bright and clean, was given her to wear.*
*Revelation 19:7–8*

Leader Guide

# Money Matters

### Ice Breaker

Have paper and pencils available for this activity. Invite participants who don't know one another to introduce themselves. If possible, serve coffee and a light snack as you begin, and keep the atmosphere relaxed. Help visitors, especially, feel welcome.

### Money—Gift of God

1. Invite a volunteer to read the opening paragraphs.

a. Have everyone find Genesis 2:8–14. Ask the question, then ask the participants to watch for answers as you read the text aloud. Accept reasonable responses drawn from the text. Here Moses clearly describes an idyllic, beautiful creation that God gave freely and in love to His human creatures, Adam and Eve.

b. Romans 1:25 cuts to the heart of the matter. Do we love the creations or the Creator? Our idolatry (Ephesians 5:5) shows itself in covetousness (Romans 7:7–8), spiritual arrogance, and worry (1 Peter 5:6–7).

2. Have volunteers read the thumbnail sketches. Then begin the discussion by sharing the person with whom you identify and a brief explanation. Don't call on anyone directly, but ask for volunteers to add their own observations.

### Financial Pitfalls

1. This question gets quite personal. Again, you may want to prime the pump by answering first yourself. Don't monopolize the conversation, however.

2. Read 1 Peter 1:18–21 aloud.

a. The metaphor Peter uses comes from the slave market of his day. When a slave was "redeemed," the price paid bought freedom.

Christ, Peter says, has redeemed us—not with silver or gold, but with something infinitely more precious, His own blood! Help participants remember that this blood covers even sins of idolatry, greed, and covetousness.

b. Let participants comment.

## Financial Planning

This course includes weekly assignments designed to help participants apply the lesson truths to their financial lives. Explain this and make it clear that this assignment will remain personal and private. No one will know if they do it or not. However, God's Word is powerful and effective (Hebrews 4:12). He wants to use it to transform our attitudes and our approaches to financial decisions, just as He uses that Word to transform our life's other attitudes and behaviors (Romans 12:1–2). In light of His powerful promises, this course *can* change individual lives! Encourage participants to make full use of this opportunity.

Will a pink Cadillac appear by magic on the driveway? Will a long-lost great uncle die and leave a fortune to erase all future mortgage payments? Probably not. But like the people of Israel at the Red Sea, we can "stand still and see . . . [what the LORD] will accomplish" (Exodus 14:12 NKJV) *in* us, first of all, and then *through* us as we place our financial well-being in His hands (1 Peter 5:7).

## Conclusion

Close with the hymn and prayer from the Study Guide.

# Making Money

### Ice Breaker

Lead the group in reading the paragraph and discussing the question. If conversation turns toward specific problems at work, with individual co-workers, or with particular investments, encourage the group to stick with more generally applicable challenges.

### Financial Lifestyle

1. Let group members speculate together. All of the women, except perhaps Wendy, probably struggle with money-making issues.

2. Spend more time here. Give participants time to think and jot down individual responses before they go on to discuss their challenges aloud. Do not call on anyone during the discussion. Rather, let volunteers raise issues. Remember that for most people in our culture talking about money carries a strong taboo.

### Money-Making and Its Meaning

1. Work together to summarize the texts. In 2 Thessalonians 3:6–15, Paul cautions against laziness and relying on the good will of others, particularly other believers, or financial support. The apostle commands honest work and urges that the church admonish able-bodied members who can work but don't. In Colossians 3:23–24, Paul encourages believers to work whole-heartedly because in serving other people, we serve our Lord Jesus.

a. Based on these texts, Christians can dedicate all their work to God. We can offer each day's work to Him as an offering of praise, a way of worshiping.

b. Participants who have completed the course *Faith at Work* from this Heart and Soul series will recognize the doctrine of vocation. Draw upon their knowledge and upon the knowledge of others in the course who may have studied the concept. Accept responses to the questions drawn from the text.

2. People in our culture do tend to value those who earn high wages more than those whose earnings barely cover their expenses. Ask for examples.

a. Jesus died for both the basketball player and the clerk. Each person has inestimable worth in God's eyes, regardless of their respective salaries.

b. Let volunteers share instances.

3. Both sets of questions in a and b could evoke confession of sins—sloth, theft in not performing one's job with due diligence, or idolatry in valuing money more than God's calling to service.

4. This question should crystallize the confession suggested in the previous question. Do not explain away or try to excuse the sins revealed here. Do, however, move directly into the next section, where you will apply the Gospel to the sins the Law has revealed.

## My Savior, My Worth

1. You might point out that in the original Greek of the New Testament, Ephesians 1:1–14 is one long sentence. It's almost as though Paul writes with so much zeal and excitement that he can't pause to take a breath. This is Good News indeed!

a. In verses 7 and 14, we again encounter the picture or metaphor of redemption we saw in the last session.

b. Accept responses drawn from the text. Focus especially on verse 4, which indicates that God chose us before our birth, even before the world's creation. We were chosen "in Him," Christ, not on our own merits. Verse 6 continues this idea, revealing that we are accepted in the One He loves—again, in Christ.

2. Let participants comment as they contemplate the immense love of God that foresaw their sins of idolatry, covetousness, worry, and unbelief, but provided redemption, adoption, and an eternal inheritance anyway! What grace and love God lavished on us!

## Financial Planning

Call attention to the assignment. Each lesson builds on the last, so encourage group members to follow through at home after each week's class session.

## Conclusion

Close with the hymn and prayer from the Study Guide.

# Spending Money

## Ice Breaker

Greet participants and help everyone feel welcome. Make the list suggested in the Study Guide, adding as many categories as your group can generate (e.g., taxes, rent, interest, gifts).

## Toys, Trust, and Trinkets

Read the details about Cara, Sally, Mary, Wendy, and Irene. Then discuss the questions at the end of this section in the Study Guide.

## Money, Greed, Worry

1. Have a volunteer read 1 Kings 10:14–29 aloud.

a. Invite participants to comment, based on the text. The key to this question comes in verse 24. If time allows, have the group compare Luke 11:31. Rulers and common people far and wide heard of Solomon's wealth and his wisdom. Solomon readily admitted to all who would listen that God had put the wisdom in his heart. His wealth and wisdom thus opened doors for witness.

b. The Lord had forbidden his kings to go back to Egypt to buy national defense (the horses and chariots of Deuteronomy 17:16; 26–29). He had also forbidden multiple wives, especially foreign, pagan wives (Deuteronomy 17:17; 1 Kings 11:1–8). Solomon indulged himself anyway, gathering so much gold and silver (1 Kings 10:25) that a tax revolt split the kingdom after his death (1 Kings 12:1–19).

2. Materially prosperous, the people of Israel (the Northern Kingdom) grew more and more idolatrous and spiritually bankrupt. The prophet Amos rails against the corruption, injustice, drunkenness, greed, and especially the idolatry of the people, particularly the women. An "equal opportunity" prophet, Amos saw that the wives and mothers in Israel instigated and participated in the nation's apostasy as thoroughly as the husbands and fathers. Gender would exempt no one from punishment when it came.

3. This question provides an opportunity to point out that when we "fear, love, and trust in God above everything else," we obey God and live in harmony with Him. However, anytime we revere, honor, love, or trust our money or our possessions more than God, we disobey; we dishonor Christ and justly deserve His punishment.

4. Discuss both parts of this question with the group, drawing out volunteers.

5. In Matthew 6:25–34, Jesus comforts the hearts of His hearers with the heavenly Father's wisdom and care. While we may not want to admit it, worry grows out of sins and unbelief. Refusing to trust the Lord's love and His promises, we chase after self-made solutions to our fears and worries.

## Return to the Lord Your God

Use this section to apply the Gospel to sins uncovered by the Law in the first parts of this session.

1. As Amos concludes his book, he paints a picture of restoration, peace, and prosperity. He gives five promises of hope to the Lord's penitent people. Help participants apply this picture of restoration to God's promised forgiveness and peace in Christ.

2. The "treasure" (Isaiah 33:6) is a right relationship with God through Christ and the wisdom and peace that accompany that relationship made possible by Christ's cross. Let volunteers tell about the comfort this treasure affords.

## Financial Planning

Call attention to this assignment. It will lead participants through a voluntary personal exercise. Encourage everyone to work through it.

## Conclusion

Close with the hymn and prayer from the Study Guide.

# Saving Money

## Ice Breaker

Welcome all participants and help everyone feel at ease. Introduce the ice breaker and invite volunteers to share experiences with saving.

## Saving or Stockpiling

Read the experiences of Cara, Sally, Mary, Wendy, and Irene. Then invite volunteers to compare their own attitudes and practices with one or more of the examples.

## A Foolish Man, A Wise Woman

1. Call on volunteers to read each text.

a. The man in Jesus' parable lives only for himself. He leads a self-centered life, finding his peace and joy only in his material wealth. The woman Lemuel describes in Proverbs 31 lives in the light of the Lord's covenant Law. She responds to that love by showing love to others in a variety of ways, using her material blessings as a good steward of the Creator's bounty. The key to a correct understanding here is not the actions of each person, but their motivation.

b. The relationship with God through the coming Messiah created within the woman right relationships with people and wealth. The fool in Jesus' parable refuses to acknowledge God and to trust in Him as Savior. Thus, there are differing outcomes in their lives.

c. Jesus condemns the rich man for his spiritual poverty before God.

d. Invite volunteers to share.

2. a. In Proverbs 31:30, Lemuel summarizes his accolades by noting that the woman who "fears the Lord" is praiseworthy.

b. Her love for Yahweh, Israel's covenant God, shows itself in self-sacrificing love and devotion.

c. Let group members speculate. We can't know for sure, of course, but her diligence and wisdom would have helped her use credit wisely. Accept answers consistent with this observation.

3. Both questions call for self-examination and confession. You may want to volunteer your own thoughts first to stimulate further discussions. As always, rely on volunteers to comment; don't embarrass anyone by putting her on the spot.

## Conceal or Confess

1. Proverbs 28:13 promises the Lord's mercy on all penitent sinners. Ignoring, hiding, or excusing sin will never help. In Christ crucified, however, we find a gracious God. He always forgives our sins and promises to help us walk away from sin's power as well. Share this Good News with one another freely!

2. Psalm 51 repeats the promise of God's forgiveness. Verses 10–12 address in particular our Lord's promised help in amending our sinful lifestyle. He creates new hearts within us. He restores the joy of our salvation. He renews within us a steadfast heart. All of this makes our new obedience possible!

3. Let volunteers comment.

## Financial Planning

Once again call attention to the benefits of doing the suggested homework.

## Conclusion

Close with the hymn and prayer from the Study Guide.

# Giving Money

### Ice Breaker

Welcome participants, especially visitors, and make any necessary introductions. Then introduce today's icebreaker questions. Let volunteers offer responses.

### Giving Money

Read the descriptions regarding the giving habits of Cara, Sally, Mary, Wendy, and Irene. With which of these women do participants most readily identify? Ask volunteers to explain their choices.

### Stingy, Foolish, Generous

1. Let volunteers read the texts aloud and comment on them. All three passages depict God as a generous, open-handed Father who wants to bless His children.

2. While Scripture commands generosity, particularly showing concern for the poor, Solomon also cautions against giving to those who don't need it. Wisdom and discernment dictate that we not squander the dollars our Lord has entrusted to us.

3. Read the verses. James condemns especially a refusal to help fellow believers who find themselves in physical want. Furthermore, he condemns wealthy landowners who refuse to pay their workers. Such fraud, the apostle warns, receives close attention in heaven's court.

4. Talk about the questions in this section. Stop any line of conversation that confesses the sins of those not present. Rather, encourage one another to wrestle with questions of stinginess and tough love on the one hand and foolishness and generosity on the other. This discussion should culminate in a confession of various sins; it brings the Law of God forward in full force.

## The Generous Grace of God

This section, then, applies the Gospel to the sin revealed in the previous discussion.

1. a. Let volunteers read aloud sentences and phrases that describe our Lord's generous grace.

b. The "washing" and "renewal" of Titus 3:5 transform us. In our Baptism, we have become new people! We have been given new hearts—generous hearts. Made new in Christ and adopted into His family, we begin to take on the family traits—generosity among them.

2. In 2 Corinthians 9, Paul delineates instructions for an offering the believers in Corinth had volunteered to give. When they begin to lag behind in their completion of the collection, Paul reminds them gently of their commitment and of their new life in Christ Jesus.

a. Verses 8–10 and 14–15 highlight the lavish grace of God.

b. Verses 6–7 and 12 hint at the need for wise discernment in giving.

c. Verses 8–11 outline God's promises.

## Financial Planning

Call attention to this week's homework assignment. If time allows, ask a volunteer or two to share the benefits they are gaining from completing the work at home.

## Conclusion

Close with the hymn and prayer from the Study Guide.

# Seeking First the Kingdom

## Ice Breaker

Welcome group members. Explain that this session sums up all that has gone before, particularly the Gospel and its power to transform our thinking about our use of money. Then lead into the opening question.

## Cara, Sally, Mary, Wendy, Irene, and Me

Give participants time to choose one woman and reread the descriptions given in Sessions 1–5. Encourage them to jot brief notes to summarize each point they would want to make in a heart-to-heart talk about money—getting, spending, saving, and giving it. If some participants are able to reference appropriate Bible texts, encourage them to do so.

## Come to the Wedding

1. Both Isaiah texts describe God's offer of salvation, freely given. Isaiah 52:3 uses the redemption metaphor we have seen elsewhere in this course. We have been redeemed not with money, but by the death of Christ our Savior. Isaiah 55:1 uses a banquet metaphor. Here the finest foods and wines are given free of charge; this, too, represents our Savior-God's generous salvation.

2. Read the passages from Revelation and accept descriptions of the marriage feast based on the texts. Note the descriptions similar to those from Isaiah in the previous question.

3. As you read Jesus' parable together, note that in first-century Palestine the king would have provided the wedding garment to his guests. Thus, the guest in verse 11 who wore his own clothes insulted the king by refusing his gift. Similarly, our heavenly Father robes us in Christ's own righteousness. Clothed in Christ, we stand blameless before God. The robe of righteousness is God's gift to us!

## The Lord, My Source

1. Let volunteers share their joy in the gracious gifts of God as each of the passages describes them.

2. Again, let volunteers share.

3. Invite participants to return to the "talking points" memo they began earlier. Before, they wrote points of Law. Now they are to add the Gospel, based on the questions and texts presented here.

## Financial Planning

Encourage participants to continue the plans they have begun.

## Conclusion

Close by asking volunteers to lead the group in praying the prayers they have written in the final activity. Then read together the italicized words from Revelation that conclude the Study Guide.